# GASTRITIS HEALIN
## FOR NEWLY D

**50+ Healthy, Gastritis-friendly Recipes to Soothe the Immune System, Heal the Stomach and Improve Digestive Health**

# Dr. Tate Mandara

# Table of Contents

**INTRODUCTION**...................................... 6

**CHAPTER ONE**...........................................8

    WHAT IS GASTRITIS?................................. 8

    TYPES OF GASTRITIS................................. 9

    CAUSES AND TRIGGERS OF GASTRITIS...12

    SYMPTOMS AND DIAGNOSIS OF
    GASTRITIS.................................................. 14

    FOODS TO EAT AND AVOID FOR
    GASTRITIS.................................................. 16

    IMPACT OF DIET ON GASTRITIS................. 19

    TIPS FOR COOKING AND PREPARING
    GASTRITIS-FRIENDLY MEALS..................... 21

**CHAPTER TWO**..................................... 24

    BREAKFAST RECIPES................................ 24

        Cinnamon Pear Oatmeal...........................24

        Blueberry Oatmeal Smoothie.................... 25

        Almond Butter Banana Wrap.................... 27

        Eggs & Toast Breakfast Box......................28

        Tropical Oatmeal....................................... 30

        Turkey Breakfast Sausage........................ 31

        Nutty Breakfast Cereal.............................. 33

        Breakfast Smoothie................................... 34

**CHAPTER THREE**................................. 36

    LUNCH RECIPES...................................... 36

        Baked Cod with Brussels Sprouts.............36

        Salmon and Vegetable Stir-Fry................. 37

        Turkey and Avocado Wrap........................ 39

Vegetable and Lentil Soup........................ 40

Baked Turkey Meatballs........................42

Quinoa Stuffed Bell Peppers....................43

Greek Style Tuna Salad........................... 45

**CHAPTER FOUR...................................... 48**

DINNER RECIPES.................................48

Broccoli Soup Cream.............................. 48

Baked Cod with Tomato and Olive Relish. 49

Sweet Potato and Lentil Curry................. 50

Tofu Pesto Pasta...................................51

Quinoa and Black Bean Casserole.......... 52

Grilled Eggplant Lasagna........................54

Turkey Meatballs with Zucchini Noodles... 55

Grilled Chicken with Sweet Potato Mash.. 57

**CHAPTER FIVE....................................60**

SIDES.............................................. 60

Sweet Potato Wedges............................60

Greek Yogurt Cucumber Salad................. 62

Fennel and Arugula Salad........................63

Cucumber Avocado Salsa........................64

Mashed Yuca........................................ 65

White & Wild Rice Pilaf........................... 66

Baked Fruit...........................................67

Ginger Carrot Soup................................ 68

**CHAPTER SIX.....................................70**

SNACKS............................................ 70

Coconut Clouds.....................................70

Almond Flour Crackers........................... 71

Banana and Walnut Energy Bites............. 73

Carrot and Hummus Dip............................ 74
Cottage Cheese and Pineapple............... 75
Fruit Jelly................................................76
Pretzel Sticks.......................................... 77

**CHAPTER SEVEN**...................................... 80
FISH & SEAFOODS....................................80
Grilled Prawn Skewers............................80
Seared Scallops...................................... 81
Baked Halibut with Herbs........................82
Baked Salmon..........................................83
Coconut Fish Sticks................................ 85
Mediterranean Baked Trout......................86
Herb-Roasted Sea Bass.......................... 88
Crab Cakes.............................................. 89

**CHAPTER EIGHT**.......................................**92**
DESSERT RECIPES................................... 92
Marmalade.............................................. 92
Vanilla Poached Pears............................ 93
Chia Seed Chocolate Pudding..................95
Coconut Milk Rice Pudding......................96
Banana Bread Muffins..............................97
Peach and Almond Crumble..................... 99
Vanilla Rice Pudding............................... 100
Watermelon Sorbet................................. 101
Peanut Butter Cookies............................ 103

**7-DAY MEAL PLAN**....................................**106**
Day 1......................................................106
Day 2......................................................106
Day 3......................................................106

Day 4.......................................................107
Day 5.......................................................107
Day 6.......................................................107
Day 7.......................................................107
**CONCLUSION**.......................................**110**

# INTRODUCTION

Tessy's journey with gastritis brought unexpected challenges, from constant discomfort to a rollercoaster of dietary confusion. Newly diagnosed, she embarked on a mission to find relief and reclaim her joy in eating. The Gastritis Healing Cookbook became her compass through this uncharted territory.

With each recipe, Tessy discovered a delightful balance of flavors tailored to soothe her sensitive stomach. The Blueberry Oatmeal Smoothie became her morning ritual, easing her into the day with a burst of antioxidants. The salmon and Vegetable Stir-Fry brought vibrancy to her lunch, offering a savory escape from bland, gastritis-triggering meals.

Dinners transformed into moments of culinary joy. The Tofu Pesto Pasta became a staple, comforting yet gentle on her stomach. Tessy found solace in the desserts too – the watermelon Sorbet satisfied her sweet tooth without causing discomfort.

As Tessy embraced this gastritis-friendly culinary adventure, she not only found relief but also a renewed sense of control over her health. The cookbook wasn't just a collection of recipes; it became Tessy's guide to healing, providing the flavors and nourishment she needed to thrive despite her gastritis diagnosis.

# CHAPTER ONE

## WHAT IS GASTRITIS?

Gastritis is an inflammation of the stomach lining, a condition that can cause discomfort and impact digestive health. The stomach lining, essential for protecting the stomach from the acidic environment it creates for digestion, becomes irritated and inflamed in gastritis. This inflammation can be acute, resulting from sudden and severe injury, or chronic, developing gradually over time. Common symptoms include abdominal pain, nausea, vomiting, and a feeling of fullness.

Various factors contribute to gastritis, such as infections, long-term use of certain medications, excessive alcohol consumption, and stress. Comprehending the underlying reason is essential for efficient handling. While treatment often involves medication, adopting a gastritis-friendly diet can play a pivotal role in alleviating symptoms and promoting healing. Avoiding irritants and incorporating gentle, nourishing foods can contribute to the overall well-being of individuals dealing with gastritis.

# TYPES OF GASTRITIS

Gastritis encompasses various types, each characterized by specific causes, symptoms, and implications for digestive health.

**Acute Gastritis**: This type involves sudden inflammation, often linked to factors like infection, stress, or the use of nonsteroidal anti-inflammatory drugs (NSAIDs). It typically resolves with treatment.

**Chronic Gastritis**: Unlike its acute counterpart, chronic gastritis develops gradually and can persist over an extended period. It may result from infections like Helicobacter pylori, autoimmune disorders, or long-term NSAID use.

**Erosive Gastritis**: This form involves erosion of the stomach lining, leading to open sores. It can result from long-term NSAID use, excessive alcohol consumption, or other irritants.

**Nonerosive Gastritis**: In contrast to erosive gastritis, nonerosive gastritis doesn't cause open sores but still involves inflammation. It can be linked to infections, autoimmune conditions, or chronic bile reflux.

**Hypertrophic Gastritis**: This rare type involves thickening of the stomach lining, potentially leading to blockages in the digestive tract. Autoimmune factors may contribute.

**Granulomatous Gastritis**: Characterized by the formation of granulomas in the stomach lining, this type is often associated with Crohn's disease or sarcoidosis.

**Radiation Gastritis**: Exposure to radiation therapy, often in the context of cancer treatment, can lead to inflammation of the stomach lining.

Understanding the specific type of gastritis is crucial for effective management. Treatment may involve addressing underlying causes, lifestyle changes, medications, or, in severe cases, surgery. A tailored approach considering the type and individual circumstances is essential for managing gastritis effectively.

# CAUSES AND TRIGGERS OF GASTRITIS

Gastritis, characterized by inflammation of the stomach lining, can result from various causes and triggers, influencing both acute and chronic forms of the condition. The primary causes include:

**Helicobacter pylori Infection**: This bacterium is a common culprit for gastritis. It can weaken the protective lining of the stomach and trigger inflammation.

**Regular Use of NSAIDs**: Nonsteroidal anti-inflammatory drugs (NSAIDs), such as aspirin or ibuprofen, can irritate the stomach lining and contribute to the development of gastritis, particularly in chronic users.

**Excessive Alcohol Consumption**: Alcohol can erode the stomach lining, leading to inflammation. Chronic alcohol abuse is a significant risk factor for gastritis.

**Autoimmune Reactions**: In some cases, the immune system mistakenly attacks the cells of the stomach lining, causing inflammation. This autoimmune response is associated with chronic gastritis.

**Bile Reflux**: When bile flows back into the stomach from the small intestine, it can lead to irritation and inflammation of the stomach lining.

**Infections and Viruses**: Gastritis can also be triggered by viral infections, such as herpes simplex virus or cytomegalovirus, as well as other bacterial or fungal infections.

**Stress**: While stress alone may not directly cause gastritis, it can exacerbate symptoms and contribute to inflammation in individuals already predisposed to the condition.

Understanding these causes helps in adopting preventive measures and developing targeted treatments to manage gastritis effectively. Lifestyle modifications, such as reducing NSAID use, moderating alcohol consumption, and addressing infections, play a crucial role in preventing and alleviating gastritis symptoms.

# SYMPTOMS AND DIAGNOSIS OF GASTRITIS

Newly diagnosed individuals with gastritis may experience various symptoms that signal inflammation of the stomach lining. Common symptoms include:

**Upper Abdominal Pain**: Many people with gastritis feel pain or discomfort in the upper part of the abdomen, often described as burning or gnawing.

**Nausea and Vomiting**: Gastritis can lead to feelings of nausea, which may be accompanied by vomiting in some cases.

**Indigestion**: Digestive discomfort, bloating, and a sensation of fullness, especially after meals, are frequent symptoms.

**Loss of Appetite**: Gastritis can result in a diminished desire to eat, leading to unintended weight loss.

**Bloating and Belching:** Excessive gas, bloating, and belching may occur due to disrupted digestive processes.

Diagnosing gastritis typically involves a thorough examination of symptoms, medical history, and lifestyle factors by a healthcare professional. Endoscopy is a common diagnostic procedure where a flexible tube with a camera is used to examine the stomach lining. Biopsies may be taken during endoscopy to determine the cause of inflammation. Additionally, blood tests can assess for H. pylori infection, and imaging studies may be employed for further evaluation. Early diagnosis and appropriate management can alleviate symptoms and prevent complications in individuals newly diagnosed with gastritis.

# FOODS TO EAT AND AVOID FOR GASTRITIS

For individuals newly diagnosed with gastritis, adopting a suitable diet is crucial for managing symptoms and promoting stomach lining healing. Here's a brief guide on foods to eat and avoid:

**Foods to Eat:**

**High-Fiber Foods**: Whole grains, fruits, and vegetables can aid digestion and promote overall stomach health.

**Lean Proteins**: Opt for lean sources of protein such as poultry, fish, and tofu, which are easier on the stomach.

**Probiotics**: Incorporate yogurt, kefir, and other probiotic-rich foods to support a healthy gut microbiome.

**Herbal Teas**: Non-acidic herbal teas like chamomile or ginger tea can have soothing effects on the stomach.

**Foods to Avoid:**

**Spicy and Acidic Foods**: These can irritate the stomach lining, exacerbating gastritis symptoms.

**Caffeine and Alcohol**: Both can increase stomach acid production and worsen inflammation.

**Fatty and Fried Foods**: High-fat meals can delay stomach emptying and intensify discomfort.

**Citrus Fruits**: Oranges, lemons, and other citrus fruits are acidic and may irritate the stomach.

Individuals should tailor their diet based on personal tolerances and preferences, aiming for a balanced and nourishing approach to alleviate gastritis symptoms.

It's advisable to consult with a healthcare professional or a registered dietitian for personalized dietary recommendations.

# IMPACT OF DIET ON GASTRITIS

Understanding the impact of diet is paramount for those newly diagnosed with gastritis. A carefully curated diet plays a pivotal role in alleviating symptoms and promoting the healing of the stomach lining.

A diet rich in nutrients, low in irritants, and easy to digest can significantly reduce the inflammation associated with gastritis.

**Balanced Nutrition**: Consuming a well-balanced diet ensures that the body receives essential nutrients for overall health, supporting the healing process.

**Avoiding Irritants**: Eliminating or minimizing foods and beverages that trigger irritation, such as spicy or acidic items, can prevent exacerbation of gastritis symptoms.

**Promoting Healing**: Including foods known for their anti-inflammatory properties, such as fruits, vegetables, and lean proteins, contributes to the healing of the stomach lining.

**Personalized Approach**: Recognizing individual triggers and preferences is crucial. Some may find relief with small, frequent meals, while others might benefit from specific dietary exclusions.

By adopting a diet tailored to individual needs and sensitivities, those newly diagnosed with gastritis can actively contribute to managing their condition and improving their overall well-being. It's advisable to consult with healthcare professionals or dietitians for personalized guidance.

## TIPS FOR COOKING AND PREPARING GASTRITIS FRIENDLY MEALS

Cooking and preparing gastritis-friendly meals involves thoughtful choices to support digestive health and minimize irritation. Here are essential tips:

1. **Selecting Lean Proteins**: Opt for lean protein sources like poultry, fish, and tofu, which are easier to digest than fatty cuts of meat.

2. **Incorporating Whole Grains**: Choose whole grains like brown rice and quinoa over refined grains to provide fiber without causing digestive distress.

3. **Embracing Low-Acidity Foods**: Favor non-citrus fruits, non-tomato-based sauces, and mild spices to reduce acidity and potential irritation.

4. **Cooking Methods**: Opt for gentle cooking methods such as baking, steaming, or grilling instead of frying to retain nutrients without adding excess fats.

5. **Portion Control**: Consuming smaller, well-distributed meals throughout the day can prevent overloading the digestive system, promoting better digestion.

6. **Hydration with Care**: Choose beverages like herbal teas and water, avoiding those high in caffeine or acidity that might trigger symptoms.

7. **Mindful Eating**: Eating slowly, chewing thoroughly, and being mindful of individual triggers can enhance the overall dining experience and aid digestion.

8. **Experimenting Sensibly**: Gradually reintroduce foods to identify personal triggers, allowing for a customized gastritis-friendly meal plan.

Adopting these tips empowers individuals with gastritis to enjoy flavorful, nourishing meals while supporting their digestive wellness. It's crucial to consult healthcare professionals for personalized advice based on individual health needs.

# CHAPTER TWO

## BREAKFAST RECIPES

### Cinnamon Pear Oatmeal

**Serving**: 1

**Cooking Time**: 10 minutes

**Ingredients**:
- 1/2 cup rolled oats
- 1 cup water
- 1/2 pear, diced
- 1/2 teaspoon ground cinnamon
- 1 teaspoon honey (optional)

**Preparation**:

1. In a small saucepan, bring the water to a boil.

2. Add the rolled oats and diced pear, reduce the heat, and simmer for 5-7 minutes until the oats are cooked.

3. Stir in the ground cinnamon and honey (if using).

4. Take off the heat source and allow it to cool down a bit before serving.

**Nutritional Value**:
Calories: 250
Carbohydrates: 50g
Protein: 5g
Fat: 3g
Fiber: 7g

# Blueberry Oatmeal Smoothie

**Serving**: 1
**Preparation Time**: 5 minutes

**Ingredients**:

- 1/2 cup rolled oats
- 1 cup almond milk
- 1/2 cup blueberries
- 1 tablespoon honey
- 1/2 teaspoon vanilla extract

**Preparation**:

1. In a blender, combine the rolled oats and almond milk. Let it sit for 5 minutes.

2. Add the blueberries, honey, and vanilla extract.

3. Blend until smooth.

4. Pour into a glass and serve.

**Nutritional Value**:

Calories: 280

Carbohydrates: 55g

Protein: 7g

Fat: 4g

Fiber: 8g

# Almond Butter Banana Wrap

**Serving**: 1

**Preparation Time**: 5 minutes

**Ingredients**:

• 1 whole wheat tortilla

• 2 tablespoons almond butter

• 1 banana, sliced

**Preparation**:

1. Spread the almond butter evenly over the whole wheat tortilla.

2. Place the sliced banana on top of the almond butter.

3. Roll up the tortilla and slice it in half.

**Nutritional Value**:

Calories: 320

Carbohydrates: 45g

Protein: 8g

Fat: 14g

Fiber: 7g

# Eggs & Toast Breakfast Box

**Serving**: 1

**Cooking Time**: 10 minutes

**Ingredients**:

•2 eggs

•2 slices whole grain bread

•1 teaspoon olive oil

•Salt and pepper to taste

**Preparation**:

1. Heat the olive oil in a non-stick skillet over medium heat.

2. Crack the eggs into the skillet and cook to the desired doneness.

3. Toast the whole grain bread slices.

4. Serve the eggs with the toasted bread.

**Nutritional Value**:
Calories: 320
Carbohydrates: 30g
Protein: 18g
Fat: 14g
Fiber: 6g

# Tropical Oatmeal

**Serving**: 1

**Cooking Time**: 10 minutes

**Ingredients**:
- 1/2 cup rolled oats
- 1 cup coconut milk
- 1/4 cup diced pineapple
- 1/4 cup diced mango
- 1 tablespoon shredded coconut

**Preparation**:

1. In a saucepan, combine the rolled oats and coconut milk.

2. Cook over medium heat, stirring occasionally, for 5-7 minutes or until the oats are tender.

3. Stir in the diced pineapple and mango.

4. Sprinkle with shredded coconut before serving.

**Nutritional Value:**

Calories: 320

Carbohydrates: 45g

Protein: 5g

Fat: 14g

Fiber: 6g

# Turkey Breakfast Sausage

**Serving**: 1

**Cooking Time**: 15 minutes

**Ingredients**:

•4 oz ground turkey

•1/2 teaspoon dried sage

•1/4 teaspoon salt

•1/4 teaspoon black pepper

•1/4 teaspoon fennel seeds

•1/4 teaspoon paprika

**Preparation**:

1. In a bowl, combine the ground turkey, dried sage, salt, black pepper, fennel seeds, and paprika.

2. Form the mixture into small patties.

3. Heat a non-stick skillet over medium heat and cook the patties for 5-7 minutes on each side or until fully cooked.

**Nutritional Value**:
Calories: 180
Carbohydrates: 0g
Protein: 22g
Fat: 10g
Fiber: 0g

# Nutty Breakfast Cereal

**Serving**: 1

**Preparation Time**: 5 minutes

**Ingredients**:
- 1/2 cup low-acid granola
- 1/2 cup almond milk
- 1/4 cup mixed nuts (almonds, walnuts, pecans)

**Preparation**:

1. In a bowl, combine the low-acid granola and almond milk.

2. Top with mixed nuts.

**Nutritional Value**:

Calories: 320

Carbohydrates: 35g

Protein: 8g

Fat: 18g

Fiber: 6g

## Breakfast Smoothie

**Serving**: 1

**Preparation Time**: 5 minutes

**Ingredients**:

- 1/2 cup plain yogurt
- 1/2 cup ripe banana
- 1/2 cup strawberries
- 1/4 cup spinach
- 1/2 cup almond milk

**Preparation**:

1. Combine all the ingredients in a blender.

2. Blend until smooth.

3. Pour into a glass and serve.

**Nutritional Value**:

Calories: 250

Carbohydrates: 40g

Protein: 10g

Fat: 5g

Fiber: 7g

The nutritional value of this recipe will vary based on the specific portion sizes and ingredients used. However, a typical serving may provide approximately

# CHAPTER THREE

## LUNCH RECIPES

### Baked Cod with Brussels Sprouts

**Serving**: 1

**Cooking Time**: 20 minutes

**Ingredients**:

- 4 oz cod fillet
- 1 cup Brussels sprouts
- 1 tablespoon olive oil
- Salt and pepper to taste

**Preparation**:

1. Preheat the oven to 375°F (190°C).

2. Place the cod fillet and Brussels sprouts on a baking sheet.

3. Drizzle with olive oil and season with salt and pepper.

4. Bake for 15-20 minutes or until the cod is cooked through and the Brussels sprouts are tender.

**Nutritional Value**:

Calories: 250

Carbohydrates: 10g

Protein: 25g

Fat: 12g

Fiber: 5g

# Salmon and Vegetable Stir-Fry

**Serving**: 1

**Cooking Time**: 15 minutes

**Ingredients**:

•4 oz salmon fillet

•1 cup mixed vegetables (bell peppers, snap peas, carrots)

•1 tablespoon olive oil

•1 teaspoon low-sodium soy sauce

**Preparation**:

1. Heat the olive oil in a skillet over medium-high heat.

2. Add the mixed vegetables and stir-fry for 3-4 minutes.

3. Push the vegetables to the side and add the salmon fillet to the skillet.

4. Cook the salmon for 3-4 minutes on each side or until it flakes easily with a fork.

5. Drizzle with low-sodium soy sauce before serving.

**Nutritional Value**:

Calories: 300

Carbohydrates: 15g

Protein: 30g

Fat: 15g

Fiber: 6g

# Turkey and Avocado Wrap

**Serving**: 1

**Preparation Time**: 10 minutes

**Ingredients**:

- 1 whole wheat tortilla
- 3 oz sliced turkey breast
- 1/2 avocado, sliced
- 1/4 cup mixed greens
- 1 tablespoon plain yogurt (optional)

**Preparation**:

1. Lay the whole wheat tortilla flat and layer with sliced turkey, avocado, and mixed greens.

2. Drizzle with plain yogurt if desired.

3. Roll up the tortilla and slice it in half.

**Nutritional Value**:

Calories: 280

Carbohydrates: 20g

Protein: 25g

Fat: 12g

Fiber: 8g

# Vegetable and Lentil Soup

**Serving**: 1

**Cooking Time**: 30 minutes

**Ingredients**:

•1/2 cup lentils

•2 cups low-sodium vegetable broth

•1 cup mixed vegetables (carrots, celery, zucchini)

•1/2 teaspoon dried thyme

•Salt and pepper to taste

**Preparation**:

1. In a pot, combine the lentils and vegetable broth. Bring to a boil, then reduce heat and simmer for 15-20 minutes.

2. Add the mixed vegetables and dried thyme.

3. Cook for an additional 10 minutes or until the vegetables are tender.

4. Season with salt and pepper before serving.

**Nutritional Value**:

Calories: 280

Carbohydrates: 40g

Protein: 18g

Fat: 3g

Fiber: 15g

# Baked Turkey Meatballs

**Serving**: 1

**Cooking Time**: 25 minutes

**Ingredients**:

•4 oz ground turkey

•1/4 cup rolled oats

•1/4 teaspoon dried oregano

•1/4 teaspoon garlic powder

•Salt and pepper to taste

**Preparation**:

1. Preheat the oven to 375°F (190°C).

2. In a bowl, combine the ground turkey, rolled oats, dried oregano, garlic powder, salt, and pepper.

3. Form the mixture into small meatballs and place them on a baking sheet.

4. Bake for 20-25 minutes or until the meatballs are cooked through.

## Quinoa Stuffed Bell Peppers

**Serving**: 1
**Cooking Time**: 40 minutes

**Ingredients**:
- 1 bell pepper
- 1/4 cup quinoa
- 1/2 cup low-sodium vegetable broth
- 1/4 cup diced tomatoes

- 1/4 cup chopped spinach
- 1/4 teaspoon cumin
- Salt and pepper to taste

**Preparation**:

1. Preheat the oven to 375°F (190°C).

2. Cut the top off the bell pepper and remove the seeds.

3. In a bowl, combine the quinoa, vegetable broth, diced tomatoes, chopped spinach, cumin, salt, and pepper.

4. Stuff the bell pepper with the quinoa mixture.

5. Place the stuffed bell pepper in a baking dish and bake for 30-35 minutes or until the pepper is tender.

# Greek Style Tuna Salad

**Serving**: 1

**Preparation Time**: 10 minutes

**Ingredients**:

- 1 can (5 oz) tuna, drained
- 1/4 cup diced cucumber
- 1/4 cup diced tomatoes
- 2 tablespoons diced red onion
- 1 tablespoon olive oil
- 1 tablespoon lemon juice
- 1 tablespoon chopped fresh parsley
- Salt and pepper to taste

**Preparation**:

1. In a bowl, combine the tuna, diced cucumber, diced tomatoes, diced red onion,

olive oil, lemon juice, chopped fresh parsley, salt, and pepper.

2. Toss gently to combine.

3. Serve as a salad or in a lettuce wrap.

The nutritional value of this recipe will vary based on the specific portion sizes and ingredients used. However, a typical serving may provide approximately

# CHAPTER FOUR

## DINNER RECIPES

### Broccoli Soup Cream

**Serving**: 1

**Cooking Time**: 25 minutes

**Ingredients**:
- 1 cup chopped broccoli
- 1/2 cup low-sodium vegetable broth
- 1/4 cup low-fat milk
- 1 tablespoon olive oil
- Salt and pepper to taste

**Preparation**:

1. In a pot, combine the chopped broccoli and vegetable broth. Bring to a boil, then reduce heat and simmer for 10-15 minutes

or until the broccoli is tender.

2. Use a blender to puree the broccoli and broth until smooth.

3. Return the mixture to the pot, add low-fat milk, olive oil, salt, and pepper. Heat through before serving.

# Baked Cod with Tomato and Olive Relish

**Serving**: 1
**Cooking Time**: 20 minutes

**Ingredients**:
- 4 oz cod fillet
- 1/2 cup cherry tomatoes, halved
- 1 tablespoon chopped black olives
- 1 tablespoon chopped fresh parsley
- 1 tablespoon olive oil
- Salt and pepper to taste

**Preparation**:

1. Preheat the oven to 375°F (190°C).

2. Place the cod fillet on a baking sheet.

3. In a bowl, combine the cherry tomatoes, black olives, parsley, olive oil, salt, and pepper.

4. Spoon the mixture over the cod.

5. Bake for 15-20 minutes or until the cod is cooked through.

## Sweet Potato and Lentil Curry

**Serving**: 1
**Cooking Time:** 30 minutes

**Ingredients**:
- 1/2 cup cooked lentils
- 1 small sweet potato, diced

- 1/2 cup coconut milk
- 1/2 cup low-sodium vegetable broth
- 1 tablespoon curry powder
- 1 tablespoon olive oil

**Preparation**:

1. In a pot, combine the cooked lentils, diced sweet potato, coconut milk, vegetable broth, curry powder, and olive oil.

2. Bring to a boil, then reduce heat and simmer for 15-20 minutes or until the sweet potato is tender.

# Tofu Pesto Pasta

**Serving**: 1
**Cooking Time**: 20 minutes

**Ingredients**:
- 2 oz whole-grain pasta

- 3 oz firm tofu, cubed
- 2 tablespoons pesto sauce
- 1 tablespoon grated Parmesan cheese
- 1 tablespoon pine nuts (optional)

**Preparation**:

1. Cook the whole grain pasta according to package instructions.

2. In a skillet, sauté the cubed tofu until lightly browned.

3. Toss the cooked pasta with pesto sauce and top with sautéed tofu, grated Parmesan cheese, and pine nuts.

# Quinoa and Black Bean Casserole

**Serving**: 1
**Cooking Time**: 40 minutes

**Ingredients**:

- 1/2 cup quinoa
- 1 cup low-sodium vegetable broth
- 1/2 cup black beans
- 1/4 cup diced tomatoes
- 1/4 cup diced bell peppers
- 1/4 teaspoon cumin
- Salt and pepper to taste

**Preparation**:

1. Preheat the oven to 375°F (190°C).

2. In a baking dish, combine the quinoa, vegetable broth, black beans, diced tomatoes, diced bell peppers, cumin, salt, and pepper.

3. Cover the dish with foil and bake for 30-35 minutes or until the quinoa is cooked and the liquid is absorbed.

# Grilled Eggplant Lasagna

**Serving**: 1

**Cooking Time**: 45 minutes

**Ingredients**:
- 1 small eggplant, sliced
- 1/2 cup low-acid marinara sauce
- 1/4 cup shredded mozzarella cheese
- 1 tablespoon grated Parmesan cheese
- Fresh basil leaves for garnish

**Preparation**:

1. Preheat the grill to medium heat.

2. Grill the eggplant slices for 2-3 minutes on each side.

3. In a small baking dish, layer the grilled eggplant, marinara sauce, and cheese.

4. Bake for 15-20 minutes or until the cheese is melted and bubbly.

5. Before serving, sprinkle some fresh basil leaves on top.

# Turkey Meatballs with Zucchini Noodles

**Serving**: 1
**Cooking Time**: 30 minutes

**Ingredients**:
- 4 oz ground turkey
- 1/4 cup breadcrumbs
- 1/4 teaspoon dried oregano
- 1/4 teaspoon garlic powder
- 1/2 cup low-acid marinara sauce
- 1 medium zucchini, spiralized

**Preparation**:

1. Preheat the oven to 375°F (190°C).

2. In a bowl, combine the ground turkey, breadcrumbs, dried oregano, and garlic powder. Form the mixture into small meatballs.

3. Place the meatballs on a baking sheet and bake for 20-25 minutes or until cooked through.

4. In a skillet, heat the marinara sauce and add the spiralized zucchini. Cook for 2-3 minutes or until the zucchini is tender.

5. Serve the turkey meatballs over the zucchini noodles.

# Grilled Chicken with Sweet Potato Mash

**Serving**: 1
**Cooking Time**: 30 minutes

**Ingredients**:
- 1 boneless, skinless chicken breast
- 1 medium sweet potato
- 1 tablespoon olive oil
- Salt and pepper to taste

**Preparation**:

1. Preheat the grill to medium-high heat.

2. Season the chicken breast with a small amount of salt and pepper.

3. Grill the chicken breast for about 6-7 minutes on each side or until fully cooked.

4. While the chicken is grilling, prepare the sweet potato mash:

5. Peel and chop the sweet potato into small cubes.

6. Boil the sweet potato cubes in water until tender, then drain.

7. Mash the cooked sweet potato with a fork or potato masher.

8. Season with a small amount of olive oil, salt, and pepper.

**Nutritional Value**:
Calories: 300-350
Protein: 25-30g
Carbohydrates: 20-25g

Fat: 10-15g

Fiber: 3-5g

The nutritional value of this recipe will vary based on the specific portion sizes and ingredients used. However, a typical serving may provide approximately

# CHAPTER FIVE

## SIDES

### Sweet Potato Wedges

**Serving**: 1

**Cooking Time**: 30 minutes

**Ingredients**:
- 1 medium sweet potato
- 1 tablespoon olive oil
- 1/2 teaspoon paprika
- 1/2 teaspoon garlic powder
- Salt and pepper to taste

**Preparation**:
1. Preheat the oven to 400°F (200°C).

2. After cleaning, cut the sweet potato into wedges.

3. The sweet potato wedges should be equally coated after being tossed in a basin with olive oil, paprika, garlic powder, salt, and pepper.

4. Place the wedges on a baking sheet in a single layer.

5. Bake for 25-30 minutes or until the sweet potato wedges are tender and lightly browned.

**Nutritional Value**:
Calories: 150-200
Carbohydrates: 25-30g
Protein: 2-3g
Fat: 5-7g
Fiber: 4-6g

# Greek Yogurt Cucumber Salad

**Serving**: 1

**Preparation Time**: 10 minutes

**Ingredients**:
- 1/2 cucumber, thinly sliced
- 1/2 cup Greek yogurt
- 1 tablespoon fresh dill, chopped
- 1 tablespoon lemon juice
- Salt and pepper to taste

**Preparation**:

1. In a bowl, combine the sliced cucumber, Greek yogurt, fresh dill, lemon juice, salt, and pepper.

2. Toss gently to combine.

3. Refrigerate for 10-15 minutes before serving.

# Fennel and Arugula Salad

**Serving**: 1

**Preparation Time**: 10 minutes

**Ingredients**:
- 1 cup arugula
- 1/2 fennel bulb, thinly sliced
- 1 tablespoon olive oil
- 1 tablespoon lemon juice
- Salt and pepper to taste

**Preparation**:

1. In a bowl, combine the arugula, sliced fennel, olive oil, lemon juice, salt, and pepper.

2. Toss gently to combine.

# Cucumber Avocado Salsa

**Serving**: 1

**Preparation Time**: 10 minutes

**Ingredients**:
- 1/2 cucumber, diced
- 1/2 avocado, diced
- 1/4 cup diced tomatoes
- 1 tablespoon chopped fresh cilantro
- 1 tablespoon lime juice
- Salt and pepper to taste

**Preparation**:

1. In a bowl, combine the diced cucumber, avocado, tomatoes, fresh cilantro, lime juice, salt, and pepper.

2. Toss gently to combine.

# Mashed Yuca

**Serving**: 1

**Cooking Time**: 30 minutes

**Ingredients**:
- 1 medium yuca root
- 2 tablespoons olive oil
- Salt to taste

**Preparation**:

1. Peel the yuca and cut it into chunks.

2. Boil the yuca in salted water for 20-25 minutes or until tender.

3. Drain the yuca and mash it with olive oil and salt until smooth.

# White & Wild Rice Pilaf

**Serving**: 1

**Cooking Time**: 40 minutes

**Ingredients**:
- 1/2 cup white and wild rice blend
- 1 cup low-sodium vegetable broth
- 1/4 cup chopped onions
- 1/4 cup chopped celery
- 1 tablespoon olive oil
- Salt and pepper to taste

**Preparation**:

1. In a pot, heat the olive oil over medium heat.

2. Add the chopped celery and onions, and sauté until the veggies are tender.

3. After adding, simmer the rice for 1-2 minutes.

4. Pour in the vegetable broth, bring to a boil, then reduce heat, cover, and simmer for 20-25 minutes or until the rice is tender.

## Baked Fruit

**Serving**: 1
**Cooking Time**: 25 minutes

**Ingredients**:
1 apple, cored and sliced
1 pear, cored and sliced
1 tablespoon honey
1/2 teaspoon cinnamon
1 tablespoon chopped nuts (optional)

**Preparation**:

1. Preheat the oven to 375°F (190°C).

2. Place the sliced apple and pear in a baking dish.

3. Drizzle with honey and sprinkle with cinnamon.

4. Bake for 20-25 minutes or until the fruit is tender.

5. Sprinkle with chopped nuts before serving.

## Ginger Carrot Soup

**Serving**: 1
**Cooking Time**: 40 minutes

**Ingredients**:
•6 cups carrots, chopped
•4 cups low-sodium vegetable broth
•1 tablespoon fresh ginger, grated
•1/2 teaspoon ground cinnamon

•Salt and pepper to taste

**Preparation**:

1. In a large pot, combine the chopped carrots, vegetable broth, grated ginger, and ground cinnamon.

2. Bring to a boil, then reduce heat and simmer for 25-30 minutes or until the carrots are very tender.

3. Use an immersion blender to puree the soup until smooth.

4. Season with salt and pepper before serving.

# CHAPTER SIX

## SNACKS

### Coconut Clouds

Serving: 1

Preparation Time: 10 minutes

Ingredients:
- 1/2 cup unsweetened shredded coconut
- 1/4 cup coconut oil
- 1 tablespoon honey
- 1/2 teaspoon vanilla extract

**Preparation**:

1. In a bowl, combine the shredded coconut, coconut oil, honey, and vanilla extract.

2. Mix well until the ingredients are evenly combined.

3. Use a spoon to form small balls and place them on a baking sheet.

4. Refrigerate for 10-15 minutes before serving.

# Almond Flour Crackers

**Serving**: 1
**Cooking Time**: 20 minutes

**Ingredients**:
- 1/2 cup almond flour
- 1/4 teaspoon garlic powder
- 1/4 teaspoon dried oregano
- 1/4 teaspoon salt
- 1 egg

**Preparation**:

1. Preheat the oven to 350°F (175°C).

2. In a bowl, combine the almond flour, garlic powder, dried oregano, and salt.

3. Add the egg and mix well until a dough forms.

4. Roll out the dough between two sheets of parchment paper until it is about 1/8 inch thick.

5. Use a knife or pizza cutter to cut the dough into small squares or rectangles.

6. Place the crackers on a baking sheet and bake for 10-12 minutes or until lightly browned.

**Nutritional Value**:

Calories: 150-200

Protein: 5-7g

Carbohydrates: 5-7g

Fat: 12-15g

Fiber: 2-3g

## Banana and Walnut Energy Bites

**Serving**: 1

**Preparation Time**: 15 minutes

**Ingredients**:

- 1 ripe banana, mashed
- 1/4 cup rolled oats
- 2 tablespoons chopped walnuts
- 1 tablespoon honey
- 1/2 teaspoon cinnamon

**Preparation**:

1. In a bowl, combine the mashed banana, rolled oats, chopped walnuts, honey, and cinnamon.

2. Mix well until the ingredients are evenly combined.

3. Form the mixture into small balls and place them on a plate.

4. Refrigerate for 10-15 minutes before serving.

## Carrot and Hummus Dip

**Serving**: 1

**Preparation Time**: 10 minutes

**Ingredients**:

•1 medium carrot, cut into sticks

•2 tablespoons hummus

**Preparation**:

1. Arrange the carrot sticks on a plate.

2. Serve with hummus for dipping.

# Cottage Cheese and Pineapple

**Serving**: 1

**Preparation Time**: 5 minutes

**Ingredients**:

•1/2 cup low-fat cottage cheese

•1/2 cup fresh pineapple chunks

**Preparation**:

1. Place the cottage cheese in a bowl.

2. Serve with fresh pineapple chunks.

# Fruit Jelly

**Serving**: 1

**Preparation Time**: 30 minutes

**Chilling Time**: 2 hours

**Ingredients**:

•1 cup fresh fruit juice (such as apple, pear, or grape)

•1 tablespoon agar-agar powder

•1-2 tablespoons honey or maple syrup (optional)

**Preparation**:

1. In a small saucepan, combine the fruit juice and agar-agar powder. Let it sit for 5 minutes to allow the agar-agar to soften.

2. Place the saucepan over medium heat and bring the mixture to a boil, stirring constantly.

3. Reduce the heat and simmer for 2-3 minutes until the agar-agar is completely dissolved.

4. If desired, sweeten the mixture with honey or maple syrup.

5. Pour the mixture into molds or a small dish.

6. Refrigerate for at least 2 hours or until set.

7. Once set, cut the jelly into cubes or unmold and serve.

## Pretzel Sticks

**Serving**: 1

**Preparation Time**: 30 minutes

**Cooking Time**: 15 minutes

**Ingredients**:
- 3/4 cup oat flour
- 1/2 cup tapioca flour (tapioca starch)
- 1 teaspoon baking powder
- 1 tablespoon coconut sugar (optional)
- 1/2 teaspoon salt
- 2/3 cup warm water
- Coarse salt for topping (optional)

**Preparation**:

1. Preheat the oven to 425°F (220°C) and line a baking sheet with parchment paper.

2. In a bowl, whisk together the oat flour, tapioca flour, baking powder, coconut sugar, and salt.

3. Add the warm water to the dry ingredients and mix until a dough forms.

4. Divide the dough into small pieces and roll each piece into a long, thin stick shape.

5. Place the sticks on the prepared baking sheet and sprinkle with coarse salt if desired.

6. Bake for 12-15 minutes or until the pretzel sticks are golden brown.

7. Allow to cool before serving.

# CHAPTER SEVEN

## FISH & SEAFOODS

### Grilled Prawn Skewers

**Serving**: 1

**Cooking Time**: 10 minutes

**Ingredients**:

- 4 large prawns, peeled and deveined
- 1 tablespoon olive oil
- 1 clove garlic, minced
- 1 teaspoon lemon juice
- Salt and pepper to taste

**Preparation**:

1. In a bowl, combine the olive oil, minced garlic, lemon juice, salt, and pepper.

2. Add the prawns to the bowl and toss to coat evenly.

3. Thread the prawns onto skewers.

4. Grill the prawn skewers over medium heat for 2-3 minutes on each side or until they are pink and opaque.

## Seared Scallops

**Serving**: 1
**Cooking Time**: 5 minutes

**Ingredients**:
• 3-4 large sea scallops
• 1 tablespoon olive oil
• Salt and pepper to taste

**Preparation**:
1. Pat the scallops dry with a paper towel and season with salt and pepper.

2. Heat the olive oil in a skillet over medium-high heat.

3. Add the scallops to the skillet and sear for 1-2 minutes on each side or until they are golden brown and opaque in the center.

## Baked Halibut with Herbs

**Serving**: 1
**Cooking Time**: 20 minutes

**Ingredients**:
• 1 halibut fillet
• 1 tablespoon olive oil
• 1 teaspoon fresh herbs (such as dill, parsley, or thyme)
• 1/2 lemon, sliced
• Salt and pepper to taste

**Preparation**:

1. Preheat the oven to 375°F (190°C).

2. Place the halibut fillet on a baking sheet.

3. Drizzle with olive oil and sprinkle with fresh herbs, salt, and pepper.

4. Arrange the lemon slices on top of the fillet.

5. Bake for 15-20 minutes or until the fish is opaque and flakes easily with a fork.

# Baked Salmon

**Serving**: 1
**Cooking Time**: 15-20 minutes

**Ingredients**:
- 1 salmon fillet
- 1 tablespoon olive oil

- 1/2 teaspoon dried dill
- 1/2 teaspoon garlic powder
- Salt and pepper to taste
- Lemon wedges for serving

**Preparation**:

1. Preheat the oven to 375°F (190°C).

2. Place the salmon fillet on a baking sheet. Drizzle with olive oil and sprinkle with dried dill, garlic powder, salt, and pepper.

3. Bake for 15-20 minutes or until the salmon is opaque and flakes easily with a fork.

4. Serve with lemon wedges.

# Coconut Fish Sticks

Serving: 1

Cooking Time: 20 minutes

**Ingredients**:

•4 oz white fish fillet (such as cod or haddock), cut into strips

•1/4 cup unsweetened shredded coconut

•1/4 cup almond flour

•1 egg, beaten

•1/2 teaspoon garlic powder

•1/2 teaspoon paprika

•Salt and pepper to taste

**Preparation**:

1. Preheat the oven to 400°F (200°C) and line a baking sheet with parchment paper.

2. In one bowl, combine the shredded coconut, almond flour, garlic powder,

paprika, salt, and pepper.

3. Dip each fish strip into the beaten egg, then coat it with the coconut mixture.

4. Place the coated fish strips on the prepared baking sheet.

5. Bake for 15-20 minutes or until the fish is cooked through and the coating is golden brown.

## Mediterranean Baked Trout

**Serving**: 1
**Cooking Time**: 25 minutes

**Ingredients**:
• 1 trout fillet
• 1 tablespoon olive oil
• 1/2 teaspoon dried oregano
• 1/2 teaspoon dried thyme

•1/2 teaspoon paprika

•Salt and pepper to taste

•Lemon wedges for serving

**Preparation**:

1. Preheat the oven to 375°F (190°C).

2. Place the trout fillet on a baking sheet.

3. Drizzle with olive oil and sprinkle with dried oregano, dried thyme, paprika, salt, and pepper.

4. Bake for 20-25 minutes or until the trout is opaque and flakes easily with a fork.

5. Serve with lemon wedges.

# Herb-Roasted Sea Bass

**Serving**: 1

**Cooking Time**: 20 minutes

**Ingredients**:
- 1 sea bass fillet
- 1 tablespoon olive oil
- 1 teaspoon fresh rosemary, chopped
- 1 teaspoon fresh thyme, chopped
- 1 clove garlic, minced
- Salt and pepper to taste

**Preparation**:

1. Preheat the oven to 400°F (200°C).

2. Place the sea bass fillet on a baking sheet.

3. Drizzle with olive oil and sprinkle with fresh rosemary, fresh thyme, minced garlic, salt, and pepper.

4. Bake for 15-20 minutes or until the sea bass is opaque and easily flakes with a fork.

## Crab Cakes

**Serving**: 1

**Cooking Time**: 20 minutes

**Ingredients**:
- 4 oz crab meat
- 1 tablespoon mayonnaise
- 1 teaspoon Dijon mustard
- 1 tablespoon chopped fresh parsley
- 1/4 cup almond flour
- 1 tablespoon olive oil
- Lemon wedges for serving

**Preparation**:

1. In a bowl, combine the crab meat, mayonnaise, Dijon mustard, and chopped fresh parsley.

2. Form the mixture into small patties and coat with almond flour.

3. Heat the olive oil in a skillet over medium heat.

4. Cook the crab cakes for 3-4 minutes on each side or until golden brown.

5. Serve with lemon wedges.

# CHAPTER EIGHT

## DESSERT RECIPES

### Marmalade

**Serving**: 1

**Cooking Time**: 30 minutes

**Ingredients**:
- 1 orange
- 1/4 cup honey

**Preparation**:

1. Cut the orange into small pieces, removing any seeds.

2. In a small saucepan, combine the orange pieces and honey.

3. Cook over low heat, stirring occasionally, until the mixture thickens and the orange pieces are soft.

4. Serve warm or chilled.

**Nutritional Value**:
Calories: 150
Fat: 0g
Carbohydrates: 40g
Protein: 1g

## Vanilla Poached Pears

**Serving**: 1
**Cooking Time**: 30 minutes

**Ingredients**:
- 1 pear
- 1 cup water
- 1 tbsp honey
- 1/4 tsp vanilla extract

**Preparation**:

1. In a saucepan, combine water, honey, and vanilla extract.

2. Peel the pear, leaving the stem intact, and place it in the saucepan.

3. Simmer for 15-20 minutes or until the pear is tender.

4. Serve warm or chilled.

**Nutritional Value**:
Calories: 120
Fat: 0g
Carbohydrates: 30g
Protein: 1g

# Chia Seed Chocolate Pudding

**Serving**: 1

**Cooking Time**: 4 hours (chilling time)

**Ingredients**:
- 1/4 cup chia seeds
- 1 cup almond milk
- 1 tbsp honey
- 1 tbsp cocoa powder

**Preparation**:

1. In a small bowl, whisk together the chia seeds, almond milk, honey, and cocoa powder.

2. Cover the bowl and refrigerate for at least 4 hours or overnight.

3. Serve chilled.

**Nutritional Value**:

Calories: 220

Fat: 8g

Carbohydrates: 26g

Protein: 7g

# Coconut Milk Rice Pudding

**Serving**: 1

**Cooking Time**: 30 minutes

**Ingredients**:

- 1/2 cup cooked white rice
- 1/2 cup coconut milk
- 1 tbsp honey
- 1/4 tsp vanilla extract

**Preparation**:

1. In a small saucepan, combine the cooked rice, coconut milk, honey, and vanilla extract.

2. Cook over medium heat, stirring occasionally, until the mixture thickens and the rice is tender.

3. Serve warm or chilled.

**Nutritional Value**:
Calories: 250
Fat: 10g
Carbohydrates: 36g
Protein: 4g

# Banana Bread Muffins

**Serving**: 1
**Cooking Time**: 25 minutes

**Ingredients**:
- 1 ripe banana
- 1/2 cup oat flour
- 1/4 tsp cinnamon
- 1/4 tsp vanilla extract

**Preparation**:

1. Preheat oven to 350°F.

2. Mash the banana in a bowl.

3. Add the oat flour, cinnamon, and vanilla extract to the bowl and mix well.

4. Fill a muffin tin with paper liners and pour the batter into it.

5. Bake for 20-25 minutes or until a toothpick inserted comes out clean.

**Nutritional Value**:
Calories: 180
Fat: 3g
Carbohydrates: 35g
Protein: 5g

# Peach and Almond Crumble

**Serving**: 1
**Cooking Time**: 30 minutes

**Ingredients**:
- 1 peach, sliced
- 1/4 cup rolled oats
- 1/4 cup almond flour
- 1 tbsp honey
- 1 tbsp coconut oil

**Preparation**:

1. Preheat oven to 350°F.

2. Place the sliced peach in a small baking dish.

3. In a separate bowl, mix the oats, almond flour, honey, and coconut oil.

4. Sprinkle the oat mixture over the peaches.

5. Bake for 20-25 minutes or until golden brown.

**Nutritional Value**:
Calories: 350
Fat: 20g
Carbohydrates: 38g
Protein: 6g

# Vanilla Rice Pudding

**Serving**: 1
**Cooking Time**: 30 minutes

**Ingredients**:
- 1/2 cup cooked white rice
- 1/2 cup almond milk
- 1 tbsp honey
- 1/4 tsp vanilla extract

**Preparation**:

1. In a small saucepan, combine the cooked rice, almond milk, honey, and vanilla extract.

2. Cook over medium heat, stirring occasionally, until the mixture thickens and the rice is tender.

3. Serve warm or chilled.

**Nutritional Value**:
Calories: 200
Fat: 2g
Carbohydrates: 42g
Protein: 5g

# Watermelon Sorbet

**Serving**: 1
**Cooking Time**: 5 hours (freezing time)

**Ingredients**:

•2 cups seedless watermelon, chopped

•1-2 tbsp lime juice

•1-2 tbsp honey or maple syrup (optional)

•A pinch of salt (optional)

**Preparation**:

1. Dice the watermelon into 1-inch cubes and place them in a single layer on a parchment paper-lined baking sheet.

2. Freeze the watermelon cubes for at least 5 hours or until frozen.

3. Once frozen, place the watermelon cubes in a blender or food processor.

4. Add lime juice and sweetener (if using) to the blender.

5. Blend the mixture until it reaches a smooth and creamy texture, scraping down the sides as needed.

6. Add a little salt to bring out the flavors, if you'd like.

7. Transfer the sorbet to a container and freeze for an additional 1-2 hours for a firmer texture.

**Nutritional Value**:
Calories: Approximately 100-150
Fat: 0g
Carbohydrates: 25-30g
Protein: 1g

## Peanut Butter Cookies

**Serving**: 1
**Cooking Time**: 12-15 minutes

**Ingredients**:

- 1/4 cup natural peanut butter
- 1/4 cup oat flour
- 1-2 tbsp honey or maple syrup
- 1/4 tsp vanilla extract
- A pinch of salt
- 1/8 tsp baking soda

**Preparation**:

1. Preheat the oven to 350°F.

2. In a bowl, mix the peanut butter, oat flour, honey or maple syrup, vanilla extract, salt, and baking soda until well combined.

3. Form the dough into little balls and arrange them on a parchment paper-lined baking sheet.

4. Flatten the balls with a fork, then make a crosshatch design on top.

5. Bake for 12-15 minutes or until the edges are golden brown.

7. Allow the cookies to cool before serving.

**Nutritional Value**:
Calories: Approximately 200-250
Fat: 12-15g
Carbohydrates: 15-20g
Protein: 6-8g

# 7-DAY MEAL PLAN

## Day 1

*Breakfast:* Blueberry Oatmeal Smoothie

*Lunch:* Baked Cod with Brussels sprouts

*Dinner:* Broccoli Soup Cream

*Snack:* Coconut Clouds

## Day 2

*Breakfast:* Almond Butter Banana Wrap

*Lunch:* Salmon and Vegetable Stir-Fry

*Dinner:* Baked Cod with Tomato and Olive Relish

*Snack:* Pretzel Sticks

## Day 3

*Breakfast:* Nutty Breakfast Cereal

*Lunch:* Turkey and Avocado Wrap

*Dinner:* Sweet Potato and Lentil Curry

*Snack:* Almond Flour Crackers

## Day 4

*Breakfast:* Eggs & Toast Breakfast Box

*Lunch:* Vegetable and Lentil Soup

*Dinner:* Tofu Pesto Pasta

*Snack:* Banana and Walnut Energy Bites

## Day 5

*Breakfast:* Turkey Breakfast Sausage

*Lunch:* Tuna Salad Lettuce Wraps

*Dinner:* Quinoa and Black Bean Casserole

*Snack:* Fruit Jelly

## Day 6

*Breakfast:* Tropical Oatmeal

*Lunch:* Baked Turkey Meatballs

*Dinner:* Grilled Eggplant Lasagna

*Snack:* Carrot and Hummus Dip

## Day 7

*Breakfast:* Breakfast Smoothie

*Lunch:* Quinoa Stuffed Bell Peppers

*Dinner:* Grilled Chicken with Sweet Potato Mash

*Snack:* Cottage Cheese and Pineapple

Remember to adapt portion sizes based on individual needs, and consult with healthcare professionals for personalized dietary guidance. Enjoy your gastritis-friendly meals!

# CONCLUSION

Embarking on the journey to heal from gastritis is a commendable commitment to your well-being. As we conclude this gastritis diet guide for the newly diagnosed, it's essential to acknowledge the power of nutrition in supporting your body's healing process. By choosing nourishing recipes designed to soothe and alleviate symptoms, you've taken a proactive step toward a healthier lifestyle. This diet isn't just a temporary fix; it's a sustainable approach to managing gastritis and promoting overall wellness. As you've explored a variety of delicious and healing meals throughout this guide, you've gained valuable insights into the impact of food choices on your digestive health.

Remember, this journey is unique to you, and progress may unfold at its own pace. Remain steady, pay attention to your body, and acknowledge each little accomplishment as it comes. Your future health is an investment that you will make when you stick to this gastritis-friendly lifestyle. Imagine how these dietary adjustments would improve your quality of life, and use that as daily motivation. Take pleasure in cooking and enjoying meals that improve your health in addition to tasting delicious. This diet is your ally in taking charge of your health. You are capable of doing so.

Printed in Great Britain
by Amazon

44454442R00066